BEGINNERS

GUIDE TO FOREX TRADING

Introduction to foreign exchange trading

A complete guide to master and understand the concept
of trading

Abraham Robert. C

In other to say thank you for purchasing this book, I offer the below video course and more to you as a token of appreciation.

Find the link to the bonus video courses at the end of this book

Happy Trading.

TABLE OF CONTENT

Chapter One

Overview of forex trading

The exchange of one currency for another is called forex trading, also referred to as foreign exchange or FX trading.

One of the world's most regularly traded markets is foreign exchange (FX), with daily transactions totaling around $6.6 trillion being made by individuals, corporations, and institutions.

Trading forex operates similarly to any other transaction in which you use a currency to purchase a single item. In forex trading, the market price indicates to a trader what quantity of one currency must be traded to buy another.

The market price of the GBP/USD currency pair, for instance, indicates how many US dollars are needed to purchase one pound.

Forex pair

A pair of currencies that are traded against one another is known as a forex pair. While there are many possible pairings, three of the most often used ones include the US dollar vs the Japanese yen (USD/JPY), the British pound versus the US dollar (GBP/USD), and the euro versus the US dollar (EUR/USD).

Base and quote currencies

In a currency pair, the quotation is always on the right and the base currency is always on the left. The quote currency is equal to the current quotation price of the pair, which indicates how many of the quote currency will be needed to purchase one base.

The currency of the base is perpetually equal to one. Therefore, selling one currency to purchase another is a constant in currency trading.

Pip in forex

In the world of forex, a pip is typically a single digit change in a currency pair's fourth decimal place. This means that if GBP/USD goes from $1.35361 to $1.35371, it has only moved by one pip. However, a pip is a change at the second decimal place if you are trading JPY crosses. In forex trading, a price fluctuation at the fifth decimal place is referred to as a pipette.

Lot in forex trading

Lots, or bunches of currency, are used to trade currencies and standardize foreign exchange transactions.

Lots are often quite big in forex since price changes are typically minor. A normal lot, for instance, consists of 100,000 units of the base currency.

What does buy or selling a pair of currencies mean

Purchasing a currency pair implies that you anticipate price growth, which would suggest that the base currency is becoming stronger in relation to the quotation currency. Selling a currency pair indicates that you anticipate a decline in price, which would occur if the quote currency lost value relative to the base currency.

For instance, if you believe that the pound would appreciate vs the dollar and that more dollars will be needed to purchase one pound, you would "buy" the GBP/USD pair. Alternatively, you would "sell" this pair if you believed that the value of the pound would decline in relation to the dollar, i.e., that a single pound would cost less money.

What is the spread in forex

The difference between the buy and sell prices in forex trading is known as the spread. As an example, the purchase price and sale price may be 1.3428 and 1.3424, respectively. Depending on whether you went long or short, the market price must either climb above the purchase price or decrease below the sale price for your position to be profitable.

What do foreign currency trading margin and leverage mean

The initial deposit required to initiate and sustain a leveraged position is referred to as margin. As a result, opening a transaction on EUR/USD may just need a 0.50% margin. Therefore, you only require a deposit of five hundred dollars to create a position as opposed to a total of $100,000

In order to benefit from one currency gaining or weakening versus another, traders place predictions on forex pairings. A rising price for a pair indicates that the base is becoming stronger against the quotation, while a dropping price indicates that the base is getting weaker against the quote.

This is so because when prices rise, more quotes are required to purchase a single unit of the base, and when prices decrease, fewer quotes are required to purchase a single unit of the base. As a result, traders would probably go short if the base were to weaken in relation to the quotation currency or long if it were to strengthen.

Scalping, swing, position, and day trading are a few of the most well-liked forex trading strategies.

What Move the Forex Market

Because there are several factors that might affect price changes, it can be difficult to anticipate exchange rates because the forex market is made up of currencies from all over the globe. Having said that, the forex market may be impacted by each of the following variables.

Central banks

Central banks regulate the amount of money in circulation and have the authority to declare policies that would significantly impact a currency's value.

For instance, quantitative easing, which includes adding more money to the economy, may result in a currency's price falling in proportion to the increase in supply.

News articles

Investors, including commercial banks, often prefer to place their money in economies with promising futures. As a result, when good news about a particular location reaches the markets, it will promote investment and raise the demand for the currency of that region. One may anticipate a decline in demand if unfavorable news breaks. For this reason, the stated economic health of the area that a currency represents is often reflected in it.

Market sentiment

Currency values may also be significantly influenced by market sentiment, which often responds to news events. If traders think that a currency is going in a certain way, they would trade in that direction and could persuade others to do the same, which might increase or decrease demand.

Chapter two

Type of forex order

Forex orders come in a variety of forms that traders may use to manage their positions. There are a few standard FX order types that most brokers accept, albeit they might change across brokers. Acquiring a comprehensive comprehension of these might aid traders in making suitable entries and exits from the market. Order types enable customized trading strategies that might provide the trader peace of mind.

Market orders

The market order is perhaps the most fundamental and often the first form of FX order that traders encounter. Market orders are exchanged at market, just as their name suggests.

This implies that you may trade a market order and be entered at the going rate if you want to join the forex market right away.

Market orders are often used by scalpers and day traders to enter and leave the market swiftly in line with their strategy.

Pending orders

Orders that you wish your broker to execute later, after the price hits your desired level, are known as pending orders. They are known as pending orders for this reason. You won't be able to enter a trade right away once you execute them, but the broker will approve the order. However, your order is executed as soon as the price of your currency pair hits the price you specified in your pending order.

Buy Limit Order

A buy-limit order instructs your broker to initiate a long position on your behalf if the price of your currency pair drops below a certain threshold. This arrangement has a straightforward concept.

When you purchase, you usually anticipate a price increase. However, you expect a little price reduction immediately before the price increases. This is where your buy-limit order enters. You are able to purchase at that discounted price.

Say you are keeping an eye on the EURUSD pair. Right now, it costs 1.1200. At now, the price is declining and getting closer to the 1.1100 support level.

You think that the price will return to 1.300 when it reaches this support level. In this case, it would be best to place a buy-limit order. When the price hits your limit price of 1.1100, you will be able to trade using this buy-limit order.

Saying, "Hey, broker, I want to buy this currency pair once it falls to a certain price level," is what a buy-limit order is like. However, I won't be here for very long to keep an eye on the market. This is my buy-limit order, then. When the price hits my preferred range, purchase the pair for me.

Sell Limit Order

When the price of a currency pair reaches a certain level, you may ask your broker to sell you the pair by placing a sell-stop order. When you sell a currency pair, you should ideally desire the price to drop to a lower amount. However, the price may need to reach a particular level (which might be a resistance level) before it drops, and you want to enter the trade at that higher price point. This is the point at which your sell limit order is relevant.

Going back to our EURUSD example, the EURUSD is now trading at 1.1100 and is slowly climbing. But you anticipate that the gradual ascent will only last until a precipitous fall occurs. At 1.1200, you thus put a sell limit order. This implies that before the broker executes your order, you anticipate that the price will increase to the designated limit price of 1.1200.

Buy stop order

When the price of a currency pair reaches a certain level, you may direct your broker to create a position on your behalf by placing a buy-stop order.

Suppose that a currency pair's price is presently growing. You do, however, expect that there could be barriers at other price points higher than the present one, which might lead the price to decline.

However, you anticipate that the price will continue to rise if it can get over those difficult pricing points. This is the kind of circumstance when a buy-stop order should be placed.

Assume, therefore, that the USDJPY is now trading at 150.35 and continues to rise. You believe there's reason to believe it should go up to 170.25, but there's a catch. The price level of 160.43 is a significant resistance level. You think USDJPY can easily reach the 170.25 goal, however, if the market can break past this resistance level. Thus, you place your Buy Stop order just above the point of resistance. In this manner, you aim to purchase the USDJPY pair when the price reaches that level and ride it until it reaches your objective.

Sell stop order

An order to your broker to sell a currency pair when the price drops to a certain level is known as a sell stop order. A sale stop works on a same principle as a purchase stop, but in the reverse way.

For example, you think a currency pair's price will keep dropping. However, you anticipate that it will first encounter a transient barrier before continuing to descend. In this situation, you place a sell-stop order.

Exit orders

These orders vary somewhat from the previously mentioned order kinds. This is due to the fact that the aforementioned categories are only requests to enter a transaction. In contrast, you may leave a deal with a trade exit order.

Three main categories of exit orders:

- Take Profit order
- Stop Loss order
- Trailing Stop order

Take Profit order

You may exit profitable deals using a take-profit order. It is your broker's directive to quit the transaction as soon as the price reaches a predetermined profit objective.

You may wonder why you would want to get out of a profitable deal. For all eternity, the cost will not be in your favor. The currency market operates in this manner. Prices fluctuate constantly. Also, you want to safeguard your earnings by getting out of transactions at the best feasible time rather than when the market turns against you.

Stop Loss order

You may exit lost transactions using a stop-loss order. It's your method of alerting the broker to assist you minimize losses at a certain price in case the market goes against you. Otherwise, you can lose all of your money if the deal goes against you.

For instance, at 1.1950, you bought or went long in EURUSD. You place a stop-loss order at 1.1920 in order to restrict your maximum loss. This implies that your trading platform would immediately shut out your trade for a 30-pip loss if you were completely incorrect and EURUSD sank to 1.1920 instead of rising.

Recall that trading forex involves some loss, and that a little loss is preferable than a large loss. To minimize your losses while trading the forex markets, use stop-loss orders. Move on, and take them on the chin. Some brokers may even forbid you from holding open transactions without placing a stop loss.

Trailing Stop order

There are occasions when you're winning a deal and you think the price will rise more. However, you are unaware of the potential reversal. In this case, a trailing stop order could be appropriate.

With a trailing stop order, you are telling your broker that you want your order to continue following the price by a certain amount if the price continues to move in your desired direction (up or down). The trailing stop order keeps moving in that direction while keeping the distance if the price keeps moving in your way. However, your trailing stop stays in place until the price reaches it if the price begins to reverse.

Assume for the moment that you are short EURUSD. You've already made money, and the price is dropping.

You want to maximize earnings, but you're not sure how long the price will drop before turning around.

One option is to establish a trailing stop order to trail the price by a certain amount of pip values, for example, 5 pip values. Your trailing stop order will be five pips above the current price in this manner. Additionally, the trailing stop will be five pips above the current price as long as the price declines. But your trailing stop will not move with the price as it begins to reverse. Instead, it will hold that position until the market closes to let you close out of the deal.

Ways to set up a forex order

Ordering forex may be done rather easily, depending on the broker. All major platforms should adhere to the following guidelines:

Once a deal ticket is open, choose the "Order" option.

Select the trade's direction (buy or sell).

Indicate the price level; based on whether the level is above or below the current market price, this will decide the kind of order.

Set boundaries or stops.

Give your order.

It's vital to keep in mind that before engaging in any kind of trading activity, you should get acquainted with the platform you are using. When managing or carrying out a deal, this might assist reduce any unrealistic mistakes.

Chapter three

Forex trading broker

A person or organization that makes it easier for you as a trader to purchase and sell foreign currency is known as a forex broker.

Speculating on a currency's value relative to another currency—for instance, the strength of the British pound relative to the US dollar—is known as forex trading. As a trader, you need a platform on which to speculate since you are not really taking possession of any notes or coins; rather, you are making predictions about their worth. This platform is provided by your brokerage, or broker.

How to choose a broker for foreign exchange

You truly want a forex broker you can trust since the forex market is the largest, most liquid, and often most turbulent market in the world. When selecting a foreign exchange broker, take into account the following nine factors:

- compliance to regulations
- Amounts of margin and leverage
- The commission rate and spread
- Deposits and withdrawals
- Trading platforms
- Trading hours
- The quantity of FX marketplaces accessible
- accessible educational resources
- Customer support

Compliance to regulations

When selecting a broker, the most important thing on your mind should be that they properly follow the law.

Amounts of margin and leverage

Another important consideration in your decision-making process is the amount of leverage and margin that you have access to.

Certain trading instruments come with leverage. It implies that you are basically borrowing from your broker for the bulk of the amount of your investment. You will deposit a portion of the deal's value, known as margin, when you initiate a forex trade; your broker will cover the remaining balance.

It also implies that you only need to invest a little amount of money to start a trade; yet, the whole value of the deal is used to determine your profits and losses. This implies that your margin amount may be greatly exceeded by both gains and losses.

The commission rate and spread

There are other fees associated with opening a position besides the margin rate. You also have to pay for "the spread" while trading forex.

Whenever you execute a forex transaction, the spread is the difference between the purchase and sale price. As our fee for the deal, we often charge our own spread in addition to the market spread. These fees are applicable to currency CFD trading.

The economic circumstances of the market have a major impact on the spread amounts. The spread will expand in proportion to a market's volatility in order to control it.

Deposits and withdrawals

There may be extra trading costs with several FX firms. Before deciding to do business with them, it's critical to understand what they are. Charges that are concealed may surface, so it very important you put this into consideration before choosing a broker

Trading platforms

The platform that you will use to place your real forex transaction is a tool that all forex brokers employ. However, not every broker offers the same selection of platforms, and not every platform is made equal.

Trading hours

The currency market is a 24/7 operation. Every day, people, businesses, and institutions trade currencies worth billions of dollars on the largest and most liquid market on the globe.

The main hubs for foreign exchange are London, New York, Tokyo, and Sydney; nonetheless, hundreds of different currencies from nations with very different time zones exchange hands in those locations. Because of all of this, FX is a global, round-the-clock market.

The quantity of FX marketplaces accessible

Naturally, in order to select the currency pair that best suits your trading style and approach, a forex trader wants the greatest number of currency pairings in addition to the highest number of hours accessible. This is due to the fact that every currency pair has unique benefits and drawbacks, degrees of volatility, and chances.

Accessible educational resources

It's also a good idea to choose an online broker with a wealth of forex training materials and tools. In short, the more you understand about FX trading, the more probable it is that you will be successful in your trading endeavors and maximizing your potential for profit while reducing your potential for loss.

Customer support

Naturally, no matter how effective your plan is, there will be occasions when you need assistance. Selecting an online trading broker with a strong platform is important, but you also want them to assist you with any questions you may have.

This is particularly important for forex traders since they may trade at odd hours, although many platforms are located abroad. What are their customer support hours if that is the case? When you need them, will they be able to answer your questions? When selecting a broker, don't forget to take communication channels and prompt availability into account.

Chapter Four

Forex trading session

Time really is money in the currency market. On weekdays, the forex market is open around-the-clock, but this does not indicate that you should trade forex assets all day or at any time. Because there are many currency trading sessions throughout the day, volatility fluctuates during the day. It's critical to comprehend the various forex trading sessions in order to choose the optimal trading hours and forex assets.

The Sydney, Tokyo, London, and New York sessions are the four primary trading sessions that often occur. It is customary to refer to the Sydney and Tokyo sessions as Asian sessions. For this reason, the three-session market—Asian, London, and New York—is how Forex is often referred to.

Different trading sessions

European/London session

At 0800 GMT, the London session begins, coinciding with the conclusion of the Tokyo session. With nearly 32% of all activity occurring during this session, it is the largest forex trading session. All significant financial hubs in Europe relate to London, a significant worldwide financial hub.

The end of the London session is at 1600 GMT. The London session is known for its extreme volatility and plenty of liquidity. The London session sees the largest price movements for several currency pairings.

During this session, most price increases and reversals occur. Because of their great liquidity, most currency pairings trade at very small spreads. The best currency pairings to trade during the London session are the euro and pound sterling pairs.

Additionally, traders should keep an eye out for updates from the Bank of England and the European Central

Bank, as well as significant economic data from EU statistics offices and nations like Germany, the UK, France, and Italy.

Asian session

The Sydney market opens at 2200 GMT to kick off the Asian session. Though it's called Sydney open, in reality, it's the opening hour of the financial markets in New Zealand. Up to the Tokyo close at 0800 GMT, the Asian session is in action. Thin liquidity often characterizes the Asian session, with most pairings typically trading inside a range. Additionally, because of the limited liquidity, currency pairings often trade at spreads that are comparatively larger. The early hours of the Asian session, when significant economic news announcements are planned, are when most action takes place. The Australian dollar, New Zealand dollar, and Japanese yen are the best currencies to trade during the Asian session. Additionally, news announcements from Australian, New Zealand, and Japanese central banks and statistical agencies should be closely monitored by forex traders.

And statistics offices in Japan, New Zealand, Australia, and New Zealand.

North American/New York session

While the London session is still in progress, the New York session begins at 1300 GMT. At 2100 GMT, which stands for the New Session comes to an end. There's also a lot going on in the New York session, particularly in the early hours when it coincides with the open London session. The US dollar, the most traded and powerful currency in the Forex markets, is the main driver of most fluctuations. Furthermore, the majority of news and events that affect the US dollar are usually announced in the early morning hours of New York's trading day. Early in the London/New York overlap (1300–1600 GMT), there is a lot of liquidity and volatility, and most assets have small spreads. Nevertheless, the second part of the New York session is often when liquidity and volatility start to decline. During the New York session, traders have access to all major pairs, including EURUSD, GBPUSD, USDCHF, USDJPY, USDCAD, AUDUSD, and NZDUSD, with the USD serving as the cue supplier. The US Federal Reserve is the central bank to keep an eye on, along with important US statistics like GDP, trade balance, industrial production, retail sales, and nonfarm payrolls.

What Time Is Best for Trading

You, the trader, will have to decide when is the optimum moment to trade. Your trading style, your time zone, or your availability. For example, the Asian trading session is a good choice if you want to target a small number of pip movements in a low-volatility market.

However, trading in the early hours of the New York session or during the London session is the ideal option if you desire significant price fluctuations and high volatility.

The ideal assets for you to trade will also depend on your time zone and availability. For example, you would be better off trading EUR and GBP pairings if you are available to trade during the London session, which runs from 0800 to 1200 GMT.

The common belief is that the optimal time to trade, in the absence of any restrictions, is when the several trading sessions overlap. Traders operating out of several global financial hubs are busy during these periods. Different assets may be traded with great liquidity and cheap spreads, and there is enough volatility. The London/New York active hours (1300hrs GMT – 1600hrs GMT) have the best overlap.

GET INSTANT ACCESS TO THE FREE VIDEO COURSE BY FOLLOWING THE BELOW LINK

subscribepage.io/freeforexcourse

Click or copy and paste the above link on your browser for instant access to the bonus video course.